THE STRAND OF HAIR
AMOY
Use Your Pain
My Autobiography

Book Two

Dr. Amoy D. Baker Ph.D.

Copyright © 2025 Dr. Amoy D. Baker

All rights reserved. No part of this publication may be reproduced, distributed, or transmitted in any form or by any means, including photocopying, recording, or other electronic or mechanical methods, without the prior written permission of the publisher, except in the case of brief quotations embodied in critical reviews and certain other noncommercial uses permitted by copyright law.

WHY THIS TITLE? THE STRAND OF HAIR

    THE
- S – STRENGTH
- T – TOUGHNESS
- R – RESILIENCE
- A – AGGRESSIVE
- N – NATURAL
- D – DETERMINATION

    OF HAIR

MY ABSTRACT

There is nothing wrong with being unique. Just because no one in your family hasn't done it before, doesn't mean that YOU CAN'T do it. Life tries to brush you into place but you keep sticking out. You keep on making mistakes, you keep on winning, you keep on losing, you keep on getting blamed or the one always carrying all the pain, and hurt from your past and now into your future. Even with all this, you must be determined to keep going because you realize that you are actually built for this. So many people have gone through less and could not stand. We must understand that everyone is not the same and we are all given a different path. So don't compare your pain to mine. You are your own book with each page telling its own story. Every moment, every minute, every hour, every day, every month, every year that you are still alive and breathing is you still walking and living out your story. If you are inspired, write it out too.

They might label you, they might color you, they might even try to blend you in so that you won't stand out. They might put a pin in you, to stay in the place that they want you to stay. But no matter what they do, YOU KEEP on STICKING OUT.

WHY 3 BOOKS?

I'm writing three books because sometimes healing comes in sections. It may not happen all at once. The process of healing may come in pieces. Each piece has its own mending, timing, tears, closure and victory. Consider a house being built. Each part of the house has its own specialized worker: plumber, electrician, mason, roofer, etc. The walls cannot go up until the foundation is dry.

Everything doesn't have to make sense. So take the risk because it might just help someone make the same move. Don't worry about whether it's going to work out or not. So what if only a few read your book? It only takes a few pennies to make cents (sense).

DEDICATION

HUSBAND

I dedicate this book to my husband because he was me. He made a decision to go against all odds at a young age when he chose me to be his partner and wife. He had no idea what he was doing. He was scared but still chose me. He had nothing to offer but still chose me. He was in his teens and like most young men was into boy things and had his own struggles. But he took a chance and still chose me. He could have been making the worst mistake of his life without knowing as we all often do, but he still chose me. He went against families and friends because they were both trying to protect him and didn't know or think he had what it took to take on such a great task. The funny thing was that they were right if he was JUST ANYONE. We understood the concerns but instead of ACCEPTING we chose to go against all odds and we added the phrase, (me and you against the world). From that day forward, in spite of the odds he became determined to stick with me for as long as we both shall live. We got pregnant 4 times, and had 3 sons, and he stood by me. I had a severe stroke and was on life support and he stood by me. I was crippled and in a wheelchair and he stood by me. In my fatherlessness and motherlessness, he stood by me. In all my victories and defeats he stood by me. In tears and sorrows, he stood by me. Yes, we had fights, disagreements, and arguments just like all couples and sometimes we even wanted to leave. I can't speak for tomorrow today! HE STILL STANDS BY ME AND almost 30 years later it's still he and I against the world! So this is why I dedicate this book to the Love of my life, my soulmate my husband.

DEDICATION

TO MY THREE SONS. THE BEST THREE GIFTS OF LIFE.

God gave me three sons that I never thought I could ever have had. They are my miracles and were my impossibilities. People spoke over me and said I would never have children and God said "Yes I would". Boys are a gift to life because they also carry the gift to keep on giving life which means I will always live on through my boys. Because of my last journey, I hated men for a season and the very thing that I hated was what God brought into my life to teach me how to love again. I have seen my babies turn into boys and I'll watch my boys turn into men. They taught me how to be strong. They taught me to fight for the people that I love. They taught me that life will always bring changes. They taught me that everyone loves differently. They taught me that everyone learns differently. My children are the one thing that I will never lose as long as I shall live. These boys are my eternal gift from God. People walk out of your life and will be your exes but your children will never stop being that. No matter how far they go or how close they stay, no matter their situation good or bad, and no matter what life brings, even until death they will always be my babies because they came out of me. I see a piece of me in all three of my boys. Every time I get into a slump where I feel unloved or inadequate or when I feel like I'm not enough. One of my boys always shows up to show me the part of me that is still worth living for. I love my three sons with everything in my body. I dedicate this book to them to show them that Mama can be strong no matter what life brings. They can do it too because they are stronger than me. I had no one and God gave me one man. In life, you will feel alone but if God sends you just one person to help push you along the way move forward, and keep on moving, you've got this. Strength comes from lifting heavy weights, muscles come from how much the weights weigh. Keep on lifting, keep on pushing. Press forward through everything you can. I heard someone say a long time ago, if you never go through anything then you'll never go through anything. Boys use this book to build the determination in yourself. Also, be encouraged to stand out and be that strand for your generation.

THE STRAND OF HAIR
WHY THIS NAME FOR THE BOOK?

I am the strand of hair because I'm one of the few people who is bold and brave enough to stand out and talk about childhood abuse and release it. I encouraged healing in the lives of adults who are still children at heart. Some adults are still stuck at the age of childhood abuse. Stuck at the age where they have had the worst abuse in their life. Even though they're adults now they're just stuck in the pain and are trying to find their way out. They can be free. I am challenged to be one of the Strands that sticks out to speak about child abuse and neglect.

I dedicate this page to those who are striving to overcome. Use your pain to make yourself move and your movements will take you where you need to go. Where you end up is where God wants you to be. Honesty is freedom so set yourself free. Free yourself from the guilt and shame. If you know the real truth then you are already free. And you shall know the truth and the truth shall make you free. John 8:32

CONTENTS

Introduction 1

Chapter 1 – Secrets Revealed 3

Chapter 2 – Closure To Adopted Father 11

Chapter 3 – Closure To Adopted Mother 15

Chapter 4 – My First Love 19

Chapter 5 – Being a Wife and Mother (Surreal To Me) 23

Chapter 6 – The Military Life and On 27

Chapter 7 – The Stroke 31

Chapter 8 – The Journey To Recovery 39

Chapter 9 – Lemonade Out of Lemons 43

Chapter 10 – My Gratitude For a Second Chance At Life 47

Chapter 11 – Keep On Pressing 51

Chapter 12 – Dealing With The Truth 55

Chapter 13 – Redirecting Your Pain 59

Chapter 14 – Rebuild Yourself 63

Chapter 15 – Use Your Pain 67

About The Author 73

INTRODUCTION

In my first book, you learned a lot about my childhood. You've had a chance to see how I learned the process of pressing through pains and trials. The story will continue as you travel with me in this story of my life. This will be a new start and discovery and a new way of living in a new country. In a new world with new people. Now I am on my own trying to find my way in life since I graduated from high school. You would think that with all that I have been through as a young child maybe at some point things will get better. Now, all of my life has not been completely bad. I have met some loving people and some nice people along the way. Some wanted to help and some could not help and I have learned how to accept that struggles would not always last. There are times in your life that you will say you deserve a better life because you endured from the past. I believe that when someone has a great purpose and has endured a great test, it gives them a greater hope for a better life. Of course, I did not believe this at that time. I have already been through so much and I've gone through so much pain and hurts in my life that I just did not want to believe that. We all need to understand that if you made it this far you can endure to the end.

Sometimes in life changes are hard, but most times in life change is necessary. So don't give up as I mentioned in the first book and don't throw in the towel. Use it to wipe your tears. Every test is designed to give you a great testimony. It is not easy for any young person to know how to plan for the future or what steps to take as they start their journey to adulthood. Every day of your life you are evolving in your mind, your spirit, and your feelings. In this book, I will share how I began my journey to try to change the trajectory of my life. I was 19 years old and I realized that I have the will to make decisions about my life on my own. It was at this age that I decided that change was necessary and was now up to me to create that change and by any means necessary.

This is where that scripture really gave me the strength that I needed Philippians 4:13 "I CAN DO ALL THINGS THROUGH CHRIST WHO STRENGTHENS ME". I knew the road would be tough because I still didn't have my family by my side. This was the time in my life when I said to myself, my past will not justify my future. I made a solemn decision that I will use all the pain, struggle, and fight that got me this far to give me strength for my future no matter what comes my way. This Is why I Amoy, The Strand of Hair will show you how I USED MY PAIN. Just remember that all things are possible to him who believes 'Mark 9:23'.

I

SECRETS REVEALED

To bring closure to Book 1, I will share with you some information that was passed on to me in my second phase of life. As I started my new life I began to wonder about my birth family and I wanted answers. Not long after I graduated from high school I spoke to one of my aunts who was willing to give me more information that I was missing. This information was regarding how I was even conceived. She began to explain the very night she believed I was conceived because she was around at the time. She began to explain to me that the man who claimed to be my father was an older man compared to my birth mother. She began to explain that the man's wife had passed and the wife was her aunt, which meant they were family as he was her uncle by marriage. Please understand that this also means that he was my mother's uncle as well since they were sisters.

I was told that I had an aunt who passed away and she had another child by another man before her marriage to my presumed father. They were having a wake service one night to honor and celebrate the life of the deceased. During this time the aunt's husband who was or should have been mourning, had left the service for some time. During that time that he was gone, he went to their home where the child was being babysat by my mother. According to my aunt, after that night my mother told her sister in deep fear that the man had sex with her. My aunt mentioned that she was told that during the wake he went to the house and while my mother was sleeping with a young child beside her, the man had intercourse with her. This came about because months later she was found to be pregnant and she had to tell the truth about how she became pregnant. She mentioned that she told the man to stop but he didn't, and she was afraid to tell anyone because she would get in trouble.

Once the pregnancy was discovered my grandmother decided to try to abort the baby. This story was very surprising to me as I'd never heard it before that day. Just when I thought that I've heard all the stories about my childhood as a baby this came to my surprise. This story was very different from the story that my aunt in the first book mentioned. The missing part of my life from age 0 to 5 is still a mystery. The abortion attempt was obviously unsuccessful and my grandmother was not happy about that. My grandmother eventually decided that she did not want the baby in her home due to the embarrassment or shame of a young child having a baby. My mother decided in the best interest of the child that she would give the child to the paternal father as she deemed him to be. When she attempted to do so, she could not find him. So she left me with his sister, my aunt. I was told that one day my mother went back to my aunt to take me back and I was missing, I was sent to another aunt who explained why she could not find me. This aunt was the one who had me sweeping the yard and such. It appears that she had me the entire time until I remembered at age 6.

I can only imagine what may have been happening to me or going on with me before the time I could remember. At this point, I don't even want to know. When I first began to inquire about my life I just wanted to find myself to see who I really am. The Bible is true when it says "And you shall know the truth and it shall make you free" John 8:32. We always say sometimes it's better off not to know but to each his own and what it takes to make me free may not be the same thing that makes you free. Not all of us are comfortable with living a lie. Some people would like to live the truth in the purity for what it is, even if it's ugly. Now I put closure to the first part of my life because it no longer matters, that story has been told. I am here now to tell you about how God himself has carried me through that level to a new level. Now I can press to what comes next for me and surely that purpose really cannot die. The Scripture is true, "Love conquers a multitude of sins" 1 Peter 4:8. Understand that in life people will love you and people will hate you but they are not obligated to you. You are primarily responsible for yourself. Remember if you never go through anything then you will never go through anything. Uncover your truth and release the secrets that keep you bound so that you can live. The Bible said Jesus came that we may have life and have it more abundantly John 10:10. I do believe with all my heart but it's not enough to just have life we must learn to LIVE. Now that I've found out that I was conceived during the time of someone's death it all became clear to me. Since I know the Lord had a purpose for my life. It really didn't matter how it happened. Since I had to be here to fulfill his purpose God had to allow it by any means necessary. So now to fulfill my future I can say. IT HAD TO HAPPEN THAT WAY.

In 2018 I went through a time of feeling upset, abandoned, and depressed for some reasons. In my heart, I feel like there was so much more that should have been answered and discovered about my family. I had a lot of questions that I still did not get answered by my biological parents. I remember asking my father questions before I came to the United States.

First of all, when you are coming to America or Canada for the first time, there are lots of medical shots that are needed before entering the country. I was found to be normal in everything. I did not have any disease however, we discovered that I had sickle cell trait. I wasn't sure of what it was exactly but was told it would be ok, I was not going to die from it, so I was fine with it. The sickle cell trait was not mentioned again until I became pregnant with my first son. They wanted to make sure that my firstborn would not have the condition as well so they questioned my husband. Praise the Lord, it turned out he was completely normal so our baby would be fine. They mentioned that he may have the trait, but that he would be absolutely fine if he did. I didn't think about it for a long time I just dealt with it. All is well as long as it was not bothering me.

I wanted to investigate as to how someone could get this condition. I started to do research and found out that one of my parents would have had to have it to pass it along. I eventually caught up with some family members and found out that my biological father did not have the trait. Then I was sure that it must have been my mother so I sought after that information as well. To my surprise my mother did not have the trait either so this was very strange. None of my biological parents were known to have sickle cell traits. Where did it come from? How did I get it? The investigation continued. I was very confused and just did not know what was going on in my life again. Now at least two or three of our children had the trait so now it's very concerning to me. I really want to know who gave it to me.

Fast forward to my adopted father being sick before he passed. He came to visit me while he was still alive maybe a couple or few months before the last time I saw him. I asked for information about his medical condition when I found out that he had the sickle cell trait.

I thought that was very strange because both of my parents did not have the trait but the one person that had it was my adopted father. Hmmm. I did not say anything for a while and just kept it quiet while I pondered. My adopted father passed before I could truly get any more information so I just said well, I will never find out the truth. One day after his death, I received a call from a lady in my home country Jamaica West Indies. She said to me that my adopted father was actually my biological father and they had proof and witness of the fact. I did not believe a word that she said to me. I was completely shocked. I had never met this lady before and I was unaware of how she got my number. She mentioned that she knew my father very well and that I needed to think about it and then she hung up the phone.

My stomach dropped to my feet. My room began to spin. I just could not believe what I was hearing or what I had heard. I did not sleep that night. My adopted father had a living brother and I had his number, he kept in touch with me the whole time during the death and the sickness of my dad. I pondered on what the lady told me for quite a few weeks. One day I decided to call my uncle, my father's brother, and ask him if there was anything that I needed to know. He wanted to know what I meant and I asked him straight out.

Was that my biological father?? I asked. He paused for a few moments and then he asked me why did I ask? I said I really needed to know. He mentions that he was my father's best friend and he kept all of his secrets and he really hoped that my dad had a chance to tell me. He had begun to apologize to me for everything that had happened. Especially the way that my dad passing without being able to tell me certain things. I asked again, Well is he my father? For real?? And he said Yes! I asked him Are you sure and he said Absolutely! You are his real baby and you're the only child he ever had. You are my biological niece and I knew it all along but could not say a word. I said Uncle why didn't you tell me and why didn't Dad tell me? He said it was very complicated and that my adoption was not a mistake even though he knew that my adopted mother did not want me. He said he was determined that he was going to get his child back. I was frozen and I sat on a chair that was close by and cried so hard that I could not move. I don't even remember hanging up the phone. I just remember that somehow I made it back home and shared all this with my husband since I was at my office at the time. From that day forward I have refrained from speaking about my father and I'm not sure if I will truly have closure. My whole life seems like one big family saga. This is all too much for me even now. There are days and moments when it is hard for me to focus. I still don't know where and to whom I belong at times. I'm so glad that I have most closure to my parents. I still do have a little bit of confusion though about some unanswered questions.

At what point would my mother have met my adopted father? Because I had so many questions, my living aunt gave me the information about my biological father having sex with my mother.

I called her one day to ask her if my mother ever knew my adopted father and did she know him as well. And the answer was yes. Now I am blown away and too much to handle. At this point, I don't want to know anything else. I tried to ask her other things but she was not able to remember much. My uncle seems to not have anything else to say. I tried to ask my biological mother who is still alive. But it's very confusing. First, my biological mother and my biological father do not have the sickle cell trait but my adopted father does. He has already passed and now it comes to light that my mother and my adopted father knew each other. You and I both are still wondering what in the world is going on !?!?!!

Now here I am being the mother that I wish I had and God being the father that I wish I had on Earth. I'm just grateful for God's purpose for my life. His purpose has been fulfilled. That's why I love the Lord God Almighty because He knows all things. And He will reveal enough for me to fulfill His plan on this Earth.

So to God be the glory!! Let's put some closure to some situations.

2
CLOSURE TO ADOPTED FATHER

Let's bring some more closure to people in the first book. Starting with my adopted father. Since the last time he was mentioned in the first book, I hadn't seen him for a long time. Many years had gone by before I had seen or heard from him again. In 2003, I had a very terrible illness come up on me. There were many medical questions for my doctors and I had gotten no answers. I figured since he was my adopted father, he may have had some information about my biological medical history that I wasn't aware of. I remember as a little girl he told me that he had discovered I had the sickle cell trait. It never caused me any issues so it was never anything to really be concerned about. Due to the medical incident, I needed to find out so I began to search for him.

I went back to the city where I first saw him because I knew he had some friends there. I did run into one guy who mentioned that he had just seen him months ago and had his phone number. I was very happy hoping to get the information I needed. I eventually got in touch with him and we began to talk for a while.

It was a very bittersweet reunion. He was so happy and wanted to find out what had been going on with me, where was my life at that point, what was going on, and such. I explained to him what had medically happened to me and why I was trying to find him. Out of that conversation we had decided to begin to try to mend our relationship as father and daughter. He mentioned to me that he ended up marrying that same secretary in the first book and now has a family with her and her son. Of course, it made me a little bitter and angry, but the Lord had already given me my own family so I didn't care too much. I was still dealing with a lot of anxieties from what I had gone through with him concerning her and all the other things of my past with him, so I wasn't sure where he was at that moment. Anyway, we continued with our conversations day after day until we eventually decided that we were going to meet and get to know each other again as father and daughter. He was very excited about meeting my children, my husband, and things of that sort. He was amazed that I was still married to the same young man that he had met. He seemed very proud of me.

After much conversation, we had to deal with the elephant in the room. I asked him to talk to me about why he did what he did and I shared with him how it affected me. I had to be bold, unafraid, and confident and it surely helped me that I had a husband by my side. All of these helped as every time I asked for an explanation about something someone did to me, I ended up getting slapped, beaten, cursed, or abused. So of course, I still had anxieties and fears. But I was an adult now and had to figure out how to move past it and do what I needed to do to be free. After I asked I was amazed because he was very humbled and ashamed and willing to be open with me and honest.

He began to express a lot of remorse for what he had done. He apologized over and over again even begging me several times to forgive him. He explained that he was a sick man and that he would have never done that to me if it was another time. He told me that I was not wrong, that I did nothing wrong or anything to deserve what he had done. The remorse was very overwhelming and I burst into tears, he gave me a big hug and told me it would never and should have never happened.

He explained to me that as a young boy, he was molested as well, but that gave him no reason to do what he did to me he said. He said I was his little girl and little girls should never be hurt in that way.

I was a little concerned at first because I didn't know if he was just saying these things just to win me back. I wanted that sense of belonging and thought I would never get it. I just could not believe what I was hearing. I had never had anyone apologize to me that much or show so much regret and remorse about what they had done to me. It was amazing. I don't remember saying anything at first. I gave him a very gentle hug and told him it was okay, but in my heart, I was just shocked. I told him that I would try to forgive him and move forward but things would take time. I allowed him to talk to my husband and to my children because they were older boys at the time. My husband and I made sure my children were safe because of my insecurities with the situation. But I still felt a little nervous.

Over a couple of years, things became better and better and I was excited and happy. I started to feel like maybe I got my father back. I was happy my children were able to talk to him over the phone, face to face whenever he came into town, and it was okay as long as things were moving in a Godly manner. He was still a Pastor and doing his ministry. So a few times I allowed him to speak at my church and encourage others. The Lord did use him greatly, and that was great because I saw the change in him and prayed that his heart was really pure to the things of the Lord and I believed that it was.

A couple more years went by and then one day he called me to let me know something terrible. He was found to be with cancer and was slowly dying. It was very sad but he came to see me and my family a few more times and we spent the rest of the time just trying to make up for all we could. Not long after he became bedridden and in and out of the hospital. Long story short, he ended up passing in 2018 and it was a very sad occasion for me. We had lost out on so many times and family things together, and the one person that ever caused me pain and joy at the same time was gone. I was very mixed up for many years because I just knew there was more that I should have asked him and there were some things he wanted to share with me was unable to, but it's okay it's over now. I was able to go to his home, going in celebration and I left closure where it was. It was over, at least I was able to forgive him and give him the opportunity to tell me the truth and to ask me for forgiveness before he passed so that we both would not have been left with unforgiveness and bitterness. In a sense, it made me free and it freed him too. So I hope that he's in heaven with the Lord and this was not held against him. When you forgive someone you are not only doing it for you, you're doing it for them too. And you're also doing it so your children and grandchildren will not be bound by that bitterness of your past as well. So far he had been the one person that had ever confessed, was remorseful, and asked for forgiveness so I had to forgive in order to put real closure to it and move on. At his Homegoing ceremony I was mentioned that I was his adopted daughter but at least I was mentioned and you'll see why I said that. Now I have closure and I moved on.

3
CLOSURE TO ADOPTED MOTHER

In 2017, the Lord began to send other people to help us in ministry and it was with great joy that my vision began to come to pass. There were many trials, struggles, and financial challenges about providing and making sure our home and the church were maintained. In the middle of it all, I received a call one day that my favorite aunt on my adopted mother's side had passed away. This was very hard for me because everyone loved her. She was the first person on my adopted family side that really showed me lots of love and welcomed me into the family. After sometime I just took a break from the stress and some of the struggles of ministry and family life. It was about six months later that I received another horrible call, it was one of my cousins on the adopted side of family to let me know that my adopted mother had passed away. This was the niece that my adopted mother left me for when I needed help after the stroke. She called to let me know that Mom had died in her sleep and my world began to spin. I wasn't sure how to feel because I had spoken to her recently and had asked her about the incident as a little girl. She admitted that it was the truth. She also apologized to me for leaving in my time of need and she made sure to tell me she loved me. Now she's gone and I didn't know how to feel. I was just in total shock. The family called to let me know about family arrangements, and the date and time of the funeral. My husband and I planned everything for the trip and I was very nervous about being around the family.

We started the journey on time to see her off to be with the Lord. I had not seen that family since and have moved on with my life. I was very aware of where she was and spoke with her a few times before she passed. There were times that we talked and tried to amend what had happened but she just never admitted to certain things. By this point, I was very happy that she had the chance to talk to me so that I can clear my head, and have the truth and peace to write this book.

We arrived at the place where the funeral would be held and there were many tears of sadness and uncertainties in the air. Some family spoke and some family did not, but it did not bother me since I didn't really know most of them anyway. As the service started they, at some point, began to read her eulogy. I listened to hear the legacy she left behind and I was sure that in the list of families, I would be mentioned since I was the only daughter that she had by adoption. As we sat and listened of the family members that were named and called out, my name was not mentioned. Neither was it mentioned that she even had a child by adoption or not. It was like someone blindfolded me and took me to the bottom of the ocean. I could not believe what I did not hear. My heart sunk and my mind began to swirl. I was embarrassed and was sickened with shame. I just couldn't understand why I was not mentioned. I became very angry and bitter at the niece that prepared the program. I was the only child, how could I not have been mentioned? I was sitting there for people to see me. One of my aunts clearly knew me because she sat beside me and spoke to me before the funeral began. I saw cousins that I played with and other family members that I knew, though I did not know all of them. To this day I still don't know why my name is not mentioned. One of my aunts who went up to speak was the only one who mentioned that her sister had an adopted daughter and that was all that was said about me.

I simply wanted to fall through the ground or get up and run out of there. My husband placed his arm around me and held me close to his side and I could tell he was feeling my pain. Again someone that I try to love that did not love me back. I just couldn't make sense of it all. We left the next day and headed back home. I was in tears most of the time, very confused and lost about it all. My adopted father was at the funeral since she passed before he did. He was also confused as to what was going on and felt really bad for me. He tried to comfort me as best as he could, and said he did not understand why my name was not mentioned. I was very numb and had pain in my heart from the whole thing. I never felt welcomed or accepted by my adopted family at any point. I did carry a lot of anger and bitterness for the niece that my adopted mother had left me for during my time of need after the stroke. I was very angry at her and very angry at my adopted mother, because neither one of them seem to have cared of the way she left me. One of the cousins tried to reach out to me, which was one of her other nieces to continue our family relationship, but I just could not handle it. They ignored me and didn't pay me any attention except to talk to me so I won't feel left out but not really including me in family matters. I had told one of my aunts that I was hurt. They were trying to help me fit in a little and they did show me a little love, but I can tell there were still some reservations.

On the way home my husband comforted me the best way that he knew how, and told me that he will be my mother and father if I would allow him. This was very devastating and impacting in my life in a negative way, but I used it to be the best mother that I could be to my three sons. First I was abandoned and thrown out by my biological mother twice, then I was never really truly accepted by my adopted mother even in her death. I really needed a break at this point and I was very drained, tired, and did not want to discuss or even deal with any of the pain or hurt of the family.

I focused really hard on the ministry, my children, and my husband. I made a few friends along the way, the Lord sent me an old lady and a few other ladies to really stand by my side and support me during this time of pain. One of them was like a mother to me and now has gone home to be with the Lord and I miss her dearly. She died about two years after my adopted mother passed. It seemed like my world was falling apart. This was the same year that I asked the Lord 'Why give me a family and now they're gone?' My father died with many unanswered questions. Just like with my mother, she was able to apologize to me as well for leaving me behind and for doing things to me that were not the right things to do. In the end she was trying to repair her relationship with me as her adopted daughter, but she was already sick and ran out of time before it could really happen. We did have a good bit of time to talk, but she lived far away so we could not really bond like we should have. She was able to meet my boys before she passed so she knew she had three grandsons. At least when my adopted father passed, it was mentioned that he had an adopted daughter which was better than I can say for my mother's funeral. It seemed like in a year and a half everybody was falling apart.

I had four deaths so close to each other. It seemed like I couldn't catch my breath between them all.

4
MY FIRST LOVE

In the first book I mentioned the young man that I had started dating. With everything going on, he never left. I was still staying with the lady and the girls and was still supporting them all. Everything was still going well there, so I stayed and continued to help the youth in the church at the same time. I eventually started calling the lady mom because all the girls called her mom as well. Not long after I graduated, that young man started to pursue me even harder.

Because of the instability in my life, I really didn't want to get serious with him. I was also terrified to fall in love with anyone since I associate love with hurt, blame and pain. We spoke on the phone for a few months before we started to date officially. During the time on the phone, we became emotionally close as we began to learn things about each others family and personal traumas. We comforted each other, encouraged one another, and we became really good friends on the phone. One day he mentioned to me that he was about to get a car, and he would like to take me out on a date. It was very exciting to go on a date for the very first time. He had a cousin that was dating one of the other girls so we thought it was a good idea to double date.

It was my very first ever so I didn't know how to dress up. I wanted him to accept me exactly the way I was, because I had no way to get money to dress any better. I wore a white t-shirt and blue jeans with a black and white Bruce Lee sneakers. I made up my mind that if he didn't like my clothes then he won't accept me for who I am. I was alone, poor, abandoned, abused and broken with nothing to offer but my heart. I was afraid to love and didn't think I could be loved. The hour has come and he came to get us in the car to take us to dinner. He was dressed very impressively in his three-piece church suit. Dressed to impress and I was. Of course, I felt under dressed but I was ok. He opened the car door for me like a perfect gentleman and allowed me to sit. On the way to the restaurant, there in the back seat, he said his first words to me. He said that he loved my eyes, and that I was prettier than ever. As I blushed with a smile he continued by saying that I had a beautiful smile as well. That was the first time I ever heard someone say something nice to me about me in that way. We arrived at the restaurant and he opened the door for me again. We went in were seated and we ordered our food. After dinner we began to talk at the table about different things. Suddenly he reached over to hold my hands, I felt a really big knot gathered in my stomach, and tears came to my eyes. I began to cry and wasn't sure why everyone kept asking what was wrong and could not explain. They all thought that he did or said something to make me cry but it was not so. The truth is that I was so overwhelmed with his kindness, his touching of my hands, and his care for my needs that I believe I was feeling love for a guy for the first time. I was so ashamed that I was falling in love for the first time. I could not stop crying for a while. I thought that he was thinking that I was crazy so he would run away and not want to be with me.

After that night we talked on the phone and he kept assuring me that it was okay that I cried and he did not think I was crazy. We continued to date for a year, then he proposed to me. It was after he asked the third time before I said yes and we became engaged for another year. We bought our marriage license in December of 1996 and became m**arried** on January 2nd 1997. This was when my world changed for the good, something I never thought could happen to me, because I was afraid and truly did not know how to love.

5

BEING A WIFE AND MOTHER (SURREAL TO ME)

Once we became married, I was in shock for a while that everything was even real. Every time I felt love in my life, it was always followed by beatings or abandonment, so this was very hard for me to accept. For the first 2 years of marriage, I was waiting for him to throw me out or start beating me or something crazy.

I became pregnant and had my first son within the first year of marriage, but I was still living in disbelief and fear. First of all, I couldn't believe I was married. My husband was determined to teach me how to receive love by showing me the most love and affection that I've ever experienced in my life. Since it was still surreal to me, I didn't put my guard down out of fear. He kept on loving me through all my fears and abandonments. He joined the military so that he could provide for and care for me. He was truly my hero. It didn't matter about my struggles and tears, nor my lack of knowing how to show love; he kept on loving me.

He bought me my first car and helped me get into our first apartment back before we got married. Since I was still living with the lady who had all of us in her home, I did not have any furniture or money to get started in my new place. Since I was new to America, I did not have a job or any credit to be approved for the place. From the very beginning, he was willing to help me achieve every goal that I wanted to achieve. We both got a job at the same company and worked together for the down payment to get into the apartment. From the beginning of the relationship, we quickly realized that we were a great team. Every week that we both received our payment from our jobs, we would combine the money and save until we met our goal for the down payment to get the apartment. After we got our first place, we continued with our partnership to furnish every room. We went to the local thrift store to purchase all the furniture and then to the Dollar General for utensils and other things needed. This was a very different experience for me to have someone by my side who was willing to support and help me without compromising my body.

Meeting my husband was the single best life change that I've ever had. As mentioned above, we got married on January 2nd, 1997, and my life changed forever. My husband wanted to make sure that he gave me the life that I had never dreamed of. He was determined to show me that all things are possible if I stayed strong. He also showed me that troubles will not always last. He sacrificed his own desires and wanted to ensure that I was cared for, but I will leave that part for him to tell. The military was another great turn in my life. My husband went to basic training for ten weeks. During this time, he kept in touch with me and assured me that he would come back to get me and our son soon. After ten weeks, the basic training was over, but I could not live on the military base right away. My husband came back to our apartment to make sure we were comfortable until he was able to make proper living arrangements on the military base for us.

Before he left, I had a car that was very rusted, and you could see the road through the bottom of the car as I drove. So when my husband came back, he took me to a car dealership and bought my first new car. I was so happy because for the first time someone made a promise to me and kept it, and that was my dream come true. After a couple of days, my husband went back to the post to prepare for us, and not long after we moved in, we reunited together to begin our family journey.

6

THE MILITARY LIFE AND ON

Most of the time, I was alone with our first son. My husband was almost always on assignments. Anyone who has been in the military, I'm sure, will understand what I mean. I truly enjoyed my journey in the military. I was able to meet a lot of wonderful people. I met plenty of mothers that I could connect with and gain more knowledge of how to be a mother. I had to learn to be independent and support my husband while he was away. I learned how to handle bills and how to care for a child without any kind of motherly guidance on my part. I was given a lot of special liberty and freedom to shop in special stores, and was enjoying myself as a woman.

My husband made sure that I was in need of nothing. He provided very well for me and made sure that when he was away, I was properly secure and safe. We stayed in the military for about three years, and instead of reenlisting, we decided to exit the military so that we could properly raise our children together.

About three years into motherhood, my husband and I had our second son, and we were elated. We decided to exit the military and buy our first home in a small city where he obtained a very good city job. We were doing as good as we could as a young couple. We did not have any family around us, so we had to really work together to raise our children. At times, it became difficult, just like any other young family, but we held on. After assessing our financial situation, we decided that two children were enough, and we were happy and wanted to make sure that we stopped at two so that we could provide for both of them and go on from there. To our surprise, we became pregnant again. We were shocked, but I was extremely excited. I say I because I believe my husband went into shock about having a third child, and we were not even trying. After a couple of weeks, he became more excited than I was, and we celebrated that we were going to be parents of three children. God was giving me the family that he promised way back in the first book.

Now we have raised 3 wonderful boys, and we would not trade them for anything in the world. We worked really hard together, bought our first home, and worked together to make sure that we did our best to provide for each of them. I had gotten a job at a local day care, and it worked very well for us. For a short time, we had two incomes, and it was a great blessing. Unfortunately, in the middle of my second trimester with my last son, I became very sick and had to be put on bed rest.

Things went on okay until I was able to give birth. The birth of my handsome son went well, and now we were celebrating our third baby in this journey. I remembered where I came from, I would never have known that I would be given three sons. Imagine how I must've felt. One moment, I hated men and hated myself, and thought I would never have children because of the things my aunts said to me. I thought I was too ugly, too unattractive, not good enough, and no one would ever want me because my aunt said so.

Now look! I am so glad I did not give up, and I'm so glad I held on and believed. If I had given up and drowned myself that day, my boys would never be here. If I had given up on myself because I thought no one would want me and that I was not adequate enough, I would've never known that I could be a mother.

I really did feel like no one would ever love me, and the Lord gave me a wonderful man to show me that it does not matter what people say about you. You must make a decision that your past should not dictate your future, and you can be strong enough to push through your pain to make things happen in your life. After all, it is your life, not theirs. Which simply means they are not in control; God is. If you only believe in the courage and strength that God put inside of you, then you will understand that pain only comes to make you move.

After my last son was born, I was very happy and pleased with my new life. My husband and I started preparing to care for them the best way we could. A lot of planning and adjustments were needed to accommodate our new life. We knew we were going to need more money and some help, but we had no family around. We began to tap into our teamwork since this is where and how we began the journey together. I was so blessed to be married to a man who showed me how to love and gave me three wonderful sons to help him love me as well. My husband is truly a gift from the Lord. And since the day I was wedded to him, I promised the Lord that I would love and cherish him until I die. Not long after giving birth, we were getting ready to go home from the hospital, and to our surprise, out of nowhere, tragedy struck.

7
THE STROKE

It was one day before I was supposed to go home on May 7th, 2003, after giving birth to my last son on May 4th. My baby was doing wonderful, but I wasn't feeling too good that day. Anyway, I was well enough to go home and just thought that maybe the way I was feeling was due to giving birth. I was home for about a week, and I was having some headaches on and off that week. By the second week, I still was not feeling well, and the headaches were getting worse. My husband and I decided to go back to the hospital where I gave birth. The emergency room doctors gave me medications and told me that maybe my discomfort was due to postpartum. I've never had that before, so I asked them to explain that to me, and they did. Saying this was the first visit to the hospital after the birth.

I went home and followed the directions with my medications, but the pain got worse. My husband, being very concerned, took me to the closest urgent care the very next morning to see what they would say about the headache. As the doctor began to examine me, he asked me to close my eyes. I wasn't sure why he asked me to do that, but as I closed my eyes, he began to ask me if I felt the touch at all on my face. I told him no. He advised me to keep my eyes closed and continue to ask me do I felt a touch.

I tried my very best to feel what he was saying, but could not feel anything. I became irritable and answered, No sir. I do not feel any touch on my face. He said I could open my eyes and then asked me to excuse him for a second.

My husband was out in the lobby with our children. My husband came to the room by himself to say that he had to take the children to a friend and that he'll be right back, that the doctor feels maybe I need to go to the hospital, just for them to do further testing. I said okay. I was not aware of what was happening to me. The doctor advised me to lie down on the bed until my husband returns. This was my second visit to the doctor about the headaches in the same week. Before my husband could return to the doctor's office, they had already called the ambulance to take me to the ER.

When I arrived at the emergency room, they began to run many tests on me. After about four or five hours, they gave me more medication and sent me home again. The pain eased for a little while, but I was not sure why I still felt funny. That night, I ate dinner with my husband and then went to sleep. The next time I woke up, it was about six weeks later, on life support in the ICU. This was my third time in the hospital for the same headache, but this time was critical; I was experiencing a severe stroke.

I prefer for my husband to tell this side of the story, but this is what I remember once I was awake, alert, and able to understand. My husband explained to me that on that particular night, I went to sleep and everything was fine, and I was sleeping well. He mentioned that I woke up at some point and went to use the restroom, and then got back into bed and appeared to have fallen back asleep. Within a few minutes, he heard a gurgling sound, and he tried to see where it was coming from. He

THE STRAND OF HAIR

mentioned that I suddenly jumped up, saying I wasn't well, and for him to call the ambulance. None of this I remember, I don't recall speaking or asking him to call anyone, so apparently I was already very sick and was speaking without knowing. My husband called the ambulance, and it seems like they were there in three seconds. He said it seemed it was very fast. I vaguely remember someone asking me to sit up on the bed and asking me to look to the left side because that's where they were standing, trying to get my attention.

I do not remember what was happening in that moment, but I remember being very frustrated because I thought that I was looking to my left. I asked myself the question, Why are they asking me to do something that I know I am already doing? I remembered being very irritated because I didn't know why they were bothering me and making me feel like I didn't know what I was doing. It was a strange feeling at the moment. What was really happening was that I was looking to my right side the entire time. I did not know that my entire left side was completely crippled and I was having a severe stroke. My husband mentioned that I lie down, and not long after, they asked him to leave the room so that they could prepare me to leave for the hospital. While they were preparing me, my husband went to get the children ready to go.

My husband and my oldest son mentioned that they saw the medics taking me out of the room, and my face and my body were covered from head to toe. The house was not very big, so the hallway was very narrow. Due to the size of the hallway, they had to carry me out on a sheet that they placed under me. All the medics had to hold each corner of the sheet to make sure that I was safe while they were taking me out to the ambulance. My husband says that once they were all good to go, it seemed like they sat there in the driveway for a long time. He became very scared and wondered why they would not leave.

After many years of recovery, I went to visit that ambulance company to see if anyone would remember me and my situation that night. I was very curious to find out what took them so long to leave the driveway. Praise the Lord, one of the workers was there the day that I visited. She was very shocked because she told me that I was dead on arrival, so she was very amazed to see me. She began to explain to me the reason why they were sitting in the driveway. She said that I flat-lined three times, and every time they tried to electrically revive me, I would gasp for air. She said to me that she had never seen someone fight that hard for their life. She mentioned that they placed me on a temporary oxygen mask so that I could get some air until I arrived at the hospital.

As the story was told to me, the doctors were very confused as to what was happening to me. I was a young mother, was only 27 years old at the time, and had never had any serious medical issues, so they were very uncertain of what to do. They discovered that I was bleeding in three places in my brain, and my left side was completely gone. The medical staff did everything they could do and tried other medications that should've helped, but did not. My brain was beginning to fill up with blood, so they had to give me medicines for that too.

My husband was told a few times to leave the room as he was trying to visit because I kept experiencing seizures. He told me that he felt very helpless to watch the love of his life in that condition. It was a very scary and uncertain time for my life, and the doctors were uncertain of what to do for a little while. They eventually had a meeting, as I was told, to decide what to do about my situation. The surgeon wanted to do open brain surgery to see what was going on. Other doctors had their own opinions, such as autoimmune disease(my body is attacking itself)and other crazy things like that. They just didn't know what was going on. They eventually allowed me to rest and just gave me the best medicine they could so I could feel better while I was there. By the time I woke up, it was about six weeks later, only to realize that my entire left side was completely gone, and I did not see my children, so I was very confused. I still had all the tubes in my body, but the most beautiful thing was that when I opened my eyes and turned to my right, I saw my hero, my husband was right there.

It was him, it was his voice, it was the man that I love, sitting by my bedside every morning, every evening, whispering in my ear as if he was convinced that I could hear everything he said. It was the voice of this man that I heard right before I opened my eyes for the first time. He will tell me he loves me, he misses me. He would tell me that he knew I could hear him. He spoke to me with so much care as if I were able to respond. When he touched me, the energy from his hand radiated through my lifeless body and stimulated the function of life within me. It was my husband's voice of prayer, so our God and the partnership of them both woke me up and brought me back to life. Without God, nothing is possible, but with God through faith, all things are possible. Today, I can truly say my husband really is a man of faith who stimulated the heart of God with his compassion and love for me. The Lord God is the head of my life and my ultimate husband, Isaiah 54:5, and my husband is my earthly King that God gave me to express his intimate love for me. So long story short, I heard the voice of my husband, and the Lord God allowed me to open my eyes.

Once my eyes were opened, day after day had gone by, and I realized that I had a purpose for still being here. I began to think about my three sons and my purpose in their lives, whatever that may be. I began to use my past as a motherless child in my desire to have a dear mother to guide me along my journey. I began to think about the love that I missed out on, the encouragement of a mother that I never had, the support that I still haven't had even during the stroke. How I had wished I had a mother to talk to me and to show me how to love my children even when I'm broken physically and emotionally. That day, I decided I would be that mother, the one that I never had. I will fight for my children, and my healing was not about me. I needed to heal for my three sons so they can see their mother fight like a champion and overcome adversities. I've always told them that a winner never quits and a quitter never wins, and this wasn't the time to quit.

I decided that I have a purpose. And as I begin to walk out my plan, I choose to do it with a smile on my face. Everyone began to acknowledge the peace that they were receiving from my smile, so I used it. My smile gave others hope, my smile gave others peace, my smile taught others that nothing should take away your grace. I was hearing these things from people in the hospital where I lived for 8 months. As I was being wheelchaired to all of my therapists. I constantly got compliments about my smile, even when I was not trying to smile. My smile was my ministry in the hospital, and my smile became the reason to go down the hallways to come back to my room, showing the hallway that I did it another day. The Lord God blessed me with a smile I never knew that I had on my face for many years. Many people in my life are trying to stop the smile from coming through my face, but the Lord God found a way through my pain to bring it through with Grace. If you think you don't have anything to offer, remember that a simple smile can change the lives of people. You do not have to be rich, and you do not have to be the most beautiful or have the best body. Just give what you have left, and it will work every time. I didn't have my walk anymore. I didn't have my run anymore. I didn't even have my whole feeling on my face or my entire feeling in my lips, but I smiled anyway. Maybe my smile wasn't as beautiful as everyone but it was mine and it showed the beauty of the Lord inside me. I heard a song by Kirk Franklin that says, "Smile for me, you will look so much better if you smile". Today, I say my smile brings life to my family, and it brings hope to the people that God entrusted me to love. This is my story, and I encourage you to tell yours.

8

THE JOURNEY TO RECOVERY

My journey of healing from the stroke began in recovery at the hospital. I remember being awakened every morning for therapy. When I woke up from the stroke, my left side was completely gone, and I could neither walk nor dress myself. It seemed as if I was born over again, and I had to learn everything from the beginning. My mornings began with learning how to hold my hairbrush in my left hand and learning how to brush my hair with a brush. Since the weakness was on the left side, I needed my right side for bracing or leaning up against something. So it was very hard. I had to have an occupational therapist, a speech therapist, and a physical therapist. All of these therapists were there to help me in my recovery in the best way that they could. Every afternoon by midday, I would get a loving call from my husband while he was at work. He was out of work for a long time because he was by my side most of the time. We were running out of money and began to lose things like our car and utilities, and were unable to provide for our home. Due to my illness, of course, I could no longer work, so my husband had to take the brunt of it all.

When I was awakened from the stroke, I could hardly see out of my eyes, and I could not even move one finger on the left side of my body. After realizing that I had lost half of my body then I realized that I didn't have my children. My husband explained to me that his grandmother, mother, and his aunt had to come from Florida to get the children. He really needed to focus on supporting my healing, so he had to let them go so that I could be cared for. I was very saddened by this because I had just had my brand-new baby boy, and I felt as if I was losing out on the most important part of his life. This made me cry terribly. I understood that I could not care for my children at that time, but I was very grateful that my husband's mother was willing, able, and capable of taking care of my babies. For this, I truly appreciate her for even to this day.

I lived at the hospital for almost a year and did the best I could to walk, talk, and recover as much as I could. Even after almost a year, I was still not recovered very much. My hands, feet, left side, and brain were just terribly sick. Eventually, my insurance began to play a part in how long I was in the hospital. They began to discuss releasing me to go home, even though I was not physically ready. My physical therapist asked the doctor to give me another couple of weeks to improve, if possible. I really liked my physical therapist because he was very passionate and had a lot of faith in my healing.

My left side was completely gone, so I could not sit up on my own. The therapist had to hand-make a physical brace to hold me up and to help me walk with a walker. It was very creative, effective, and helpful. Those couple of weeks came and went very quickly, and we were still not ready. Now is the time for me to go home, and I was scared, and I could tell that my husband was very nervous, but he kept his cool for me. I had the stroke on or around May 8, 2003. And I lived in the hospital for almost a year during the entire event. During this time, my husband came every day to make sure that I was properly being cared for. He always brought me a loving smile and gentle touch. Always come into my room as if it were the first time we met. My husband always brightened up my day and gave me hope to fight every time I saw him. My children were the driving force that pushed me to be the best that I could be, even in my situation. My God was the ultimate place of peace that allowed me to know that all of this that I was going through was going to work out for my good somehow.

The day came for me to go home from the hospital, and of course, we were scared, uncertain, and frightened of how to live this new life. My husband had never been with a disabled wife. Home, as I remember, was not the same because I knew my children were not there. My mind became like a rushing wind all the way home. How am I going to kiss my husband? How am I going to make love to him? I will never be able to be a wife again. All my abilities seemed to be gone at the time. I was afraid that I would not be able to make him happy in any way. I was a great cook before the stroke. I knew how to clean my home, do our laundry, and make things that had to happen as a mother in my home. I knew how to be a mother, go grocery shopping, and help pay the bills. I knew how to bathe my children, change their diapers, and do a lot of motherly and wifely chores that I'm no longer able to do. I was petrified and almost did not want to go home because I felt inadequate and afraid.

I remembered telling my husband, Honey, if you're not able to handle this, I do understand and I will not blame you if you would like to be with someone else. I release you, because I love you, I said. I just did not want my husband to feel the pressure of life on his own with me. Three small children and the crippled wife that will make four babies that my husband would have to care for. This was all in 2003.

We arrived home, I asked my husband when will the children return? What I did not know was that he had a surprise for me. He and my adopted mother had already picked up the children in Florida the day before. The children were home with my adopted mother, waiting for me to arrive, and I was so surprised. I really wanted my babies. It was hard for me to care for myself, and my husband was having a hard time as well, as he needed to go back to work.

We agreed that my adopted mother would stay and help us with the children and such until we were able to handle things on our own. Everything seemed to have been going fine, but one morning she spoke to me and my husband and said that another family member needed her more than I did. By this point, I still could not bathe myself or feed myself. I wasn't even able to give myself my own prescriptions. I still was not able to change my baby's diapers because of my left hand. When she mentioned this to us, I cried, and we begged her not to leave. We explained to her that we needed a little more time so that I could create ways of being more independent and give my husband time to plan. She became very adamant about leaving and said she had to go and that we could not have more time. She stated that one of her nieces needs her and that we will be fine. After about a week, we took her to the train station, placed her on the train, and sent her on her way with tears and heartbrokenness.

9

LEMONADE OUT OF LEMONS

Immediately after my adopted mother left, I believe we went into survival mode. My husband and I realized that we were on our own. We began to strategize how we were going to take care of our family with me being disabled. Since my husband had to go back to work and we could not afford in-home assistance, we had to make things happen with us and our boys.

I was taking about 8 to 10 different medications at the time, and I was not able to take them on my own without assistance. My insurance allowed for a therapist to come into our home twice per week for physical therapy, and that was exciting because at least I had some help for my body.

My husband began to train my six-year-old firstborn son to assist me while he was away at work. My husband would prepare all of my medications for certain times of the day. At those times of the day, he would call my son and ask him to give them to me, which was set out. My son also had to help with his baby brothers in any way that he could.

My husband was at work in his body, but his mind and heart were at home. Eventually, with some help from a church member's advice, we decided to homeschool our children so that they could help their dad care for me. This was a very humbling time in my life. I was supposed to be the mother for my children instead they were being the fathers for me. There were times when I had to use the restroom, and my six-year-old son had to assist. Of course, I was protecting him from certain things that should be unseen to a child, but he had to assist with the walker and give me things to help myself. After my husband came home from work, he had to take care of all other necessities to ensure that we were all okay at the end of the day for bedtime, then start over the next day.

I was still recovering in a lot of ways by this point. I still was not able to walk, talk, or do anything independently on my own. Sometimes at night, I would dream that I was having a stroke again, and it would terrify me. It is safe to say that I was truly traumatized every time I lay down in that bed. Sometimes I used to envision my body going out of the home with a sheet covering my head. I can only imagine the fear in my children's hearts and the terrible thoughts that may have been going through my husband's mind.

After many months of praying and believing in my heart that I would walk again, I began to try. My middle son began to have dreams about me walking. He would come into my room and touch my hand and pray for Jesus to heal me. He had a dream that I would walk again, and that gave me hope. There were days that I would attempt to walk because I could see it in my mind that I could do it. Of course, I would fall, and my husband would run towards me with fear and terror that I would hurt myself. But because of my determination, I was still willing to keep on trying. I wanted to be independent again, so I began to use what I had left. I tried to fold laundry, and they were not very beautiful, but I was happy that I could do something. I would lean up against my kitchen counter and place chairs around with my wheelchair, just so I could try to cook for my family. I was not going to let the situation stop me from doing my very best. It was a tough time for us, but I was still determined to try to be the mother and the wife that God has called me to be. After many months of our new life that was handed to us, we began to process that I could've died. It was terrifying.

There were days upon days that I kept having flashbacks and memories of the event in my home, and did not want to continue to relive it over and over again. Eventually, my husband and I decided to buy another home to give us all a fresh start in this new journey. With God's blessing, we bought another home about 10 miles away, but in the same city. We were so excited because the house was big enough to raise our three boys, and also had stairs to aid in my physical therapy. God really moved for us and under the lemon of my mother leaving us into the lemonade of teaching us how to stand on our own and work together as a team and family. When my mother left, I thought I would just fall apart. I thought I would be a terrible mother with not knowing how to change my own baby's diaper and not being able to cook for my children and my husband. I thought that my husband would become overworked and leave us because he would've been burned out. I thought this was going to turn out very terrible for us because we didn't know how to do this on our own.

But God is faithful to watch over his children and care for us. The Bible says," That God will never leave us nor forsake us" Hebrews 13:5. Once again, the Scriptures came alive to me. It was the same Scripture that I heard under the tent that day, Psalms 27 verses 10 -14 "When my mother and my father forsake me, then the Lord will take me up, KJV." We moved into our new home in 2005 and are still there to this day as this book is being written.

10

MY GRATITUDE FOR A SECOND CHANCE AT LIFE

Once we were blessed with our new home, we immediately prayed and blessed it. We wanted to make sure that our life was protected under Jesus for the next journey. My husband had applied for a new job with the City, and we were in prayer that he would get it.

In the meantime, all three boys were being boys and growing as fast as they wanted to. We had two boys who started school. So we had to get prepared for that journey as well.

As time went on and we settled into our new home, I began to zoom in on my gratefulness for what God has done for me.

During this healing of the stroke, I've had many people who were praying for me. My faith in God increased even more because of all the things that He has already brought me through. With all that I had gone through with the stroke, I never questioned the Lord nor asked Him why that happened. All I could think of was that I needed to get better for my family. I understood that this was not something that I could do on my own. Some things were still out of my husband's and the doctor's control. I decided to focus on God because I believe that He is my healer. I was already attending a local church, and I had continued my praise and worship youth ministry with them. So I was very strong in the Lord, and I knew that all things were possible with Him. I became very passionate about doing the things of the Lord and wondered how I could do it.

I had a passion to start a church and to help people by praying for them and helping them with food and clothing, and anything that could encourage to motivate, and encourage them. I was limited in what I could do because I had no money, building, equipment, or people to help me; all I had was my family.

I began to remember a moment when I was sitting in my bed in the first house while I was pregnant with my last son. I was reading a story about a young man who was thrown into the lion's den. The story mentioned that God closed the mouth of the lion so that he would not be eaten up, and the next day, they took him out. I remember thinking to myself, this was a very interesting story, and I thought to myself that maybe I should write a book about my story. I never knew that this would come to pass; it was just a thought. About a week later, I had the stroke, and here I am now, 21 years later, writing about it.

As I remember that moment, the desire became stronger and stronger to do ministry for the Lord. Many of the things that needed to be done, I have already seen that my adopted father, who was a Pastor. I became very passionate and driven about the vision that I see of helping people and starting a church. I began to write the whole vision down on a piece of paper, and then I typed it out and began to work on it. I did not know a lot of people, but I knew enough that maybe if I let them know that I was starting a church that they would come to help. I began to pray about all the things I needed to get started, and the Lord began to provide these things for me. I started looking for a place to gather, and I found it through another pastor. Then the Lord began to bless me with chairs and equipment, and the things that I needed. In the meantime, my children were playing music with my pots and pans in my kitchen, and it would make me very upset. It wasn't long before I realized that the Lord was teaching them to play music. They became the first musicians for our church, and if you hear them, you would think that they had many years of training.

In 2009, my first ministry, Faith in Action Worship Center, was born. I knew that if this was going to work, I had to use my faith and put it into action because nothing would've happened if I focused on my limitations. My husband, being my support and my love, was with me from the very beginning, along with my three beautiful sons. We had a couple of ladies who came along, but after a long time, they left, and more people began to come. It was not easy, and some days it was only the five of us, but it was okay because we still had faith in God that one day this would work out.

II

KEEP ON PRESSING

At this point, I am dealing with a lot. All my family members were gone by way of death, but at the same time, after much thinking, I realized that I didn't have them to begin with after all. In my life's journey in dealing with the stroke, my mother abandoned me, and my father was completely absent the entire time. I had no other family to call on, but I had to call on Jesus, and he came to my rescue. My husband and my children are my family that the Lord gave me, and we are still standing without the help and support of anyone in my family. At the time of the deaths of both of my parents, I was still healing and going to the doctors for different things, like headaches and pain, and different parts of my body. The doctor's visits were mainly preventative care and to change any medication if needed to accommodate the stresses of life. The doctors were asking questions about family history, which brought to my attention to seek out my biological family.

After the stroke I went back home to Jamaica to visit. At that time, I saw aunts and some of my cousins. While I was there, I found my biological mother as well. Even though it was extremely hard, I spoke to her and loved on her as if nothing happened. After I returned back to the United

States, I pondered the conditions that I saw while I was there. Most people would think that she deserved what I saw. The conditions were not good, she was very poor and sad with the living conditions that they were in. I was never the one to render evil for evil, so I helped her and brought her to the United States to help give her a better life. It did not work as I planned because we did not get along well, but it all worked out in the end, and she was able to stay and get the better life that she wanted. In the meantime, I found out that I had other family members in the United States. I made it my best goal to find them and speak to all of them, but I decided to continue my life's journey with just my immediate family, my husband, and my sons. All the families that I found were people who were part of my pain.

This was very hard for me because even though I knew that I needed people by my side, I could not allow them in my space. I am not saying that they are the worst people in the world because they are still my family by blood. I'm just saying that I'm in a place in my life where I have control over what happens for the most part. Whatever pain and sadness that comes will be, most of the time, what I allow. There will be things that may happen in my life that I have no control over, but at least it will be the Lord who has the last word.

I am no longer being beaten up because of someone else's mistake. I am no longer being cussed out because I asked a simple question. I can eat when I want, and I can love anyone whom I place in my life. No one has control over me but the Lord himself and the earthly gift of my husband's love he cherishes for me.

I'm very glad I met this part of that family because I was eager to ask questions about my health and background that I was not aware of. I was also given pertinent information about my past that I needed to encourage myself for my future. I learned a lot about what I was like as a child as I began to speak to them. It brought back many memories as if it just happened yesterday. As some of them spoke to me, I can tell that they did not see much of me and thought that I was going to be exactly what they said I would. There is one of my cousins that I still talk to today because she seemed very understanding of my pain. She's able to speak to me about certain things and helped me to realize that I had a right to feel the way that I do. She supports me strongly in my passion for ministry and is not very surprised at all by the greatness that God has in my life.

I spoke to one of the aunts who abused me a couple of times, but it always made me feel very sad on the inside. At one point, this aunt behaved as if she did not remember the things that she had done to me, which is hard for me to believe. I recently spoke to another aunt from that side of the family, and I was okay with her, even though there were a few things that happened with her as well. I'm okay now, I'm so glad that I made it through that ordeal, and now I can write about it. I have so much to do in the next chapters of my life, and as I continue to write this book, you can stay with me in this journey.

12
DEALING WITH THE TRUTH

Here I am in my late 40s, and I'm still dealing with many things as a result of my past. Most people would like to stay to themselves. And try to forget about these things since I don't have to deal with them anymore. I'm glad for those who have convinced themselves that their past does not define their future. My truth is that as I begin the journey of life as an adult, I realize that I have still not lived most of my life in its fullness. I am still hearing many stories about my childhood that I was not aware of. Most of it does not matter anymore because I have surpassed many of the pains that I went through.

I mentioned earlier about my husband that I met during my life journey. When we met, I was in terrible shape because of all the things that I mentioned and had been through. I was very afraid to love and did not want to be hurt anymore by anyone. I spoke a lot about our beginning in chapter 4, but it did not stop there. My life journey began with this man in a time in my life when I hated every man, and I did not think I was capable of falling in love. As you can see by reading chapter 4, all things are possible with Christ. We are still married today and getting ready to celebrate almost 30 years of being together. Our children are now full-grown adults, and we now have four grandsons. I would not have believed if someone had told me when I was six years old that one day I would have children of my own.

As I mentioned, being a married woman is a journey. As I was raising my children, I had to learn to be the mother that I never had. Keep in mind, I had no mother around me to show me how to be a mother and absolutely no father to guide me along the way either. Many years since I met my husband, I would cry at every Mother's Day and Father's Day because I had no one to give a card or a special gift. Even though life sent some women along, they either passed away or they just did not work out. They had other adult children of their own. This is a void I still struggle with at times because the more I am a mother, the more I need one to call on for guidance. I have tried talking to other mothers who are older than me to learn things, and I can manage to think of some things along the way.

The Lord God has given me plenty of love to give my boys with His love and His grace. I just decided that I would be the mother that I so desired, and maybe it would be best that way because my children would receive all the love that is bottled up inside. I'm much older now and a grandmother, so I really don't have time to worry about my own feelings. It was even more challenging for me learning how to be a wife. This can still sometimes be very challenging because these things you should learn from an elder. This is hard because I don't really see a lot of examples around me. Many of you who are reading this book can relate to this feeling.

Maybe your mother has passed on to the Lord, or maybe they're just not around you or in your life. In some cases, your mother is around and you know where she is, but you just don't have a good relationship with her for one reason or another. Sometimes the worse pain we carry is for the ones that are still alive, walking around, believe in, and the ones we love. Every time you see their face and every time you hear their voice, it brings a level of pain that makes you want to crawl under a rock and disappear. Most of the time, the people who caused you the most pain are the ones closer to you, and that is hard to live with because we are already family.

There are so many unreleased pains in people walking around you, and you will never see it most of the time. Sometimes the pain comes from a mother or father or a best friend, a neighbor, or even a teacher, but it all needs to be discussed. Everybody's pain is very different, but we are all expected to keep on living. Everyone's life journey is designed differently, but you must make a decision. You may question yourself and wonder why you have to go through these things while everyone else's path seems so clear. At some point, we waste so much time watching other people and assuming that their path is clear and safe. Most people are walking around in severe pain and bitterness, and you will never know it. We all have learned how to become great disguisers.

I am going to try to encourage you to let it go. I know you think you are moving, but you are not believing as long as you're walking in the darkness of your past. Your past has become an ongoing force of disguise, so no one can rain down true love on your life. I have learned that being honest with myself has given me freedom because honesty is freedom. We have to know the truth, accept the truth, and it will make you free. The Bible said in John 8:36, "And you shall know the truth and it shall make you free".

13

REDIRECTING YOUR PAIN

As you get older in life and begin to evolve, your mind will change about things about people and especially about yourself. You think you're loving, but you're not loving at all because there are hindrances in your heart that prevent you from moving freely. The same is true; it's not enough to be alive, but you must learn to live and take advantage of the moments that life brings to be happy.

You would think I realized this after I had the stroke. The only thing I realized after the stroke was that life is short. Then I learned that if you're going to live your life, live your life in the best way that you can. Don't rob yourself of the peace you deserve and the love that you deserve because you are carrying the pain of others who don't know how to love. Give yourself permission to receive love and understand that love is very conditional. I say this because everyone will care for you, and everyone wants you in their presence, and everyone will see the love until you do something to hurt their feelings. Things will change if you don't agree with their ideas or thoughts. Things will change if you don't love them the same way they love you; therefore, love is conditional. It is based on how they perceive love and not on the way you perceive love. Love for you and me could mean just a simple hug or acknowledgment when you are around. But for others it may mean constant communication, always giving, always helping, or something of that matter. But if you cannot give love in one moment, or if you cannot make them feel better about something, then the love will change towards you. This proves my point: love is very conditional.

This is why I say in the previous chapter, honesty is freedom, because if you're honest, then they already know that what you say is what you mean. When you have been hurt so much, there comes a time when you no longer believe what anyone says, but you only believe what they show you.

Don't waste too much time. Find something or someone that you love, even if it's an animal, then redirect your energy of love in the way that you express it, and don't look for any return. Just live what you believe and stand on it. Don't expect anyone to love you and treat you the way you treat them. People always choose to love you and treat you the way they want to treat you in spite of how you love. If you are one that carries around a lot of pain, use it in a positive way. If you hate men, get a male dog or male cat and start there. You must free yourself from this hate and bitterness. Start thinking about how much love you can give a child or someone who might be in your position. It is never easy to go through pain and troubles, but it's a part of the process of life, and we must let go of the things that stop us from pursuing life.

These pages will never be enough to tell the whole story, but I can give you a little help along the way. Trials come to make you strong and to redirect you in the way you should go. I have gained a lot of strength from my past. Because of the pain that I have, I used it as a young adult to stay away from the things that have already caused me pain. I use the beatings as a reminder to listen to my children and not to take their words, feelings, and emotions for granted. I use the false accusations as a reminder to make sure that I tell the truth at all times. I used the abandonment that I felt to secure myself in the love of God and to make sure that I provide for myself in education, hard work, being dependable, and being trustworthy. This is to make sure that I create a safe space that belongs to me without depending on others. I use the rejections to remember to accept others and their ideas, and to allow others to feel that their opinion matters, even if I just listen. I use the lack of a mother and a father to be the best. But I know I'll be ok with the help and guidance of the Lord and all the elders around. Learning how to redirect your pain is a powerful empowerment for yourself. You can use it to create a new you if you try hard enough.

14

REBUILD YOURSELF

I have been saying in my writing that all things are possible with God. Now that I've gained the confidence to be a great mother and wife, I began to search out the rest of my purpose in life. I know that people have got to be the reason for the purpose that I've gone through so much, so as I begin to pursue my career and strength in ministry, I begin to flourish in the Lord. My children became a part of the music program in my church, which was great. I did not send my children to music school, so the Lord himself gave them the gift of music.

Even though I had a stroke and I was not physically able to do a lot of things with my physical body, I was always a great speaker. My husband was raised in a very quiet style of church, and I was more into the Pentecostal and charismatic type of church. But together we have a balance in the ministry, and people love the way we serve the ministry together. Because we wanted to enhance our education and relationship with the Lord, my husband and I went back to school and gained a Bachelor's degree in theology so that we could be better ministers and understand the Word for the betterment of our church. I really enjoyed learning a lot about the Lord and felt that extra pulling to continue going back-to-school and getting my Master's, then my Doctorate in Christian Counseling in 2017.

During this time, I decided to use my experience in life and my education in school as a method of encouraging my community. I started a Christian counseling program for people in my church, and therefore members of my community, at no charge. As I begin to work in ministry, I realize I really love the children. I was drawn to them because, in some strange way, I can feel their pain just by walking near them.

I started working at the day care center in my local community and completely found myself in many of the children. Yes, I saw myself in my own children as well when they were growing up, and I gave them all the love I have for others. Being in the daycare, I saw many little girls who reminded me of myself, and I just poured out my love and commitment to my classroom. After a while, I got the desire to start my own daycare, and I did. I did in-home daycare for maybe 12 years until all of my children were grown and gone off to college. As I continued in the ministry, I saw many needs that I could not help, and it made me very sad. There ware needs for housing, which was very hard for me.

Since you now know my past, I'm sure you understand. After seeing the need, I decided to open a food pantry for the families. This is what I mean by use your pain. Use it for the greater good, use your pain to free someone.

I was told many times by one of my aunts that I would never be anything and that I would never be good in my community. I was told that I was a nobody and that no one in the world would want me. I was told that I was ugly and not wanted. As I began to learn the Lord more, I realized that he created me just the way I am for His purpose and His will. I believe the

Scripture when it says that "I am fearfully and wonderfully made," Psalm 139:14.

To all the people of my past, I am moving forward, and my past will not justify my future. I am blessed and favored by the Lord. The Lord has beheld me and I am beautiful because He created me. And yes, a man married me, and he loves me more than words can say. Now I have wonderful sons and grandchildren who love me greatly. I am well educated and strong in the Lord, fighting the good fight on this journey. It's not always easy, but things will work out every time. Life would make you cry sometimes, but don't throw in the towel. Use it to wipe your tears.

15

USE YOUR PAIN

When I graduated from high school in 1995, it was a very bittersweet time for me. There were a few students who were part of the media club who were going around asking all the seniors questions. My question was, what would you like to say to your fellow classmates to take with them into the world? My answer was a phrase that I had heard on my journey, A quitter never wins and a winner never quits. I'm not sure at what point I heard that phrase. Sometimes I wonder if I even created it on my own because I haven't heard anyone saying it since. When I began to have children, I kept the phrase going in life and family. My three boys were raised with that phrase. That phrase was my motivational speech during every family meeting and any discipline for my children. I still believe that today that if we are quitters, we will never win anything, and if we are winners, then we never quit anything.

Today I have been married for 28 years and together with my husband for 30 years. Three sons who are now adults and four beautiful grandsons. Two sons are married. All three of my sons are very successful people in our community. With all that I have been through, I have learned to use my pain to push through wherever I need to go in this life and to achieve any goal I set for myself. I made a decision that my past will not justify my future, but I will use it to qualify me. I have learned how to use my pain to encourage others and to give them hope that if I can make it through, then they can too.

Whenever I meet struggles in life, I usually take a moment and remember where I come from and how I got here. The little girl I was would be in so much fear that she would run away if she could from every pain that she experienced. So now I look at her and I say Stand and fight. She would allow people to do what they wanted to her because she was afraid and didn't know what to do. Sometimes she felt like she deserved it because she must have done something wrong. Today, I would tell her you did absolutely nothing wrong. You are a young child, and you do not deserve this abuse from anyone. The adults were responsible for keeping you safe and secure; you are not your own caretaker at such a young age, so they were responsible for you. I would tell her that I'm so proud of her for being strong and fighting her way through. If I see little girl me today, I will give her a big hug and squeeze her very tightly in order for her to feel a moment of safety and love. I would probably try to take her away to a far country to help her walk away from the pain.

I would give her love and attention and the parental care that she needs. I would protect her body with everything I have in me, and I'll keep her in my arms everywhere I go. I would tell her every day that she's special and that she's valuable to someone special in the future. If I could see little girl me, I would tell her that she is worth lots of love. My life goal would be to show her and teach her to guard your heart and save it because someone is coming one day who will show you and teach you to love again. Fortunately, the little girl has gone up, and here I am writing this beautiful novel to let you see that what men cannot do, God can. I am 49 years old today, and I'm stronger than I've ever been in my life. I have gained wisdom from my pain and have obtained strength from the pressures of life. Since I became a wife and a mother, there have been more lessons taught to me, but I took them in stride. I was not always a perfect wife, but I was perfect enough for my family. I was not always the perfect mother, but I was perfect enough for my three sons. I was not always a perfect person, but perfection comes from God. Today, I am counseling many young mothers and many young children in my community. I am an influencer to many leaders, and even through all of these great accomplishments, I still struggle, but I'm moving forward. No one said life would be easy, and I am not the only one who has been through a lot of pain in their life.

I have chosen to walk this walk of transparency. Many people see me today and are deceived by the blessings in my life. My husband and I are in our second house that we bought, I have the children and grandchildren, the backyard fence, and cars that were paid for. I go on many vacations and do wonderful things with my family and friends. Things seem to be going very well with me from the outside. But there are still days and moments when the memory and the results of pain still hurt. It took many years for me to truly allow my husband to love me. But now that I know what love feels like, I want to share all. Love takes strength, love takes patience, love takes understanding, love takes compromise, love takes honesty.

One thing that I learned and am still learning is that no one can love you more than you. I have taken all the lessons in my life, and I've used them to love myself more than anyone else could. During my years of childbearing, I learned that pain can sometimes result in beautiful things. Now I celebrate with my children and my husband and many beautiful extended family and friends who love me and appreciate me for the beautiful and loving woman that I have become in spite of my pain.

I want to encourage you, as the reader of this book, to find a dark place in your heart or your mind that has caused you to lose hope in your dream or your passion. Use all of your disappointments and your pain and frustrations to unlock your next move. Remember if you're still alive then you still have a pulse. Then remember that where there is a pulse, there is life. And where there is life there is still hope.

Today, I am the Founder and CEO, working very hard in our Christian ministries. Faith in Action Worship Ministries International, Faith In Action Bible College, Community Empowerment Support Inc., and the community food pantry feed thousands of families a year. We established our ministry in 2009 and the Bible college in 2018 for the betterment and encouragement of our Christian community. I established Family Talk Consulting LLC in 2024. Because of my past, I recognized the need for food in our community, so in 2010, we connected with the North Carolina Food Bank and established our community food pantry, which is still going, with community volunteers to help. A special thanks to the volunteers for making that happen for the families.

As mentioned in my introduction, I truly honor the Lord, my husband, and my children for being the foundation of my love. And for loving all my setbacks and seasons of pain. They have watched me grow into a mighty warrior for the Lord. They have been by my side every step of the way. It was not always easy for any of us during all of my life changes, but we stand together as one family. I give all the glory to our Lord Jesus Christ, who chose me. Now I'm having happy days on this journey as well. I heard a song that says, "Troubles don't last always" (Kirk Franklin), and it is true.

In my next book, which is the third of this three-book series, you will join me in my current endeavors, from where the Lord will take me from here. There are so many things that I left out of this book, but I just wanted to give you enough to bring closure and answers to the first book and information moving forward. I am the strand of hair that will always stand out from the rest.

Remember, don't stop reading, it's not over until it's over.

ABOUT THE AUTHOR

Dr. Amoy D. Baker is a woman with a passion for reaching the world one person at a time. A native of Jamaica, Dr. Baker moved to Canada in 1990 with her missionary parents. At 15, her family relocated to America to establish a local church as part of their missionary work.

Dr. Baker attended high school and college in the United States, following in her parents' footsteps by becoming a pastor and counselor for her local church. She is the founder of Faith in Action Worship Ministries International, Community Empowerment and Support Inc., Faith and Action Bible College in Garner, NC, and Family Talk Christian Counseling.

Dr. Baker and her husband, Louis Baker, live in North Carolina and have three sons and four grandsons. Her foundational scripture is Philippians 4:13: "I can do all things through Christ, who strengthens me."

www.ingramcontent.com/pod-product-compliance
Lightning Source LLC
Chambersburg PA
CBHW050041080526
44586CB00014B/1402